SPOTLIGHT ON NATIONS

BRAZIL

NELL MUSOLF

CREATIVE EDUCATION · CREATIVE PAPERBACKS

Published by Creative Education and Creative Paperbacks
P.O. Box 227, Mankato, Minnesota 56002
Creative Education and Creative Paperbacks are imprints
of The Creative Company
www.thecreativecompany.us

Design and production by Blue Design, Inc.
Art direction by Graham Morgan
Edited by Grace Beltowski and Ana Brauer

Photographs by Getty Images/EVARISTO SA, 26, Global_Pics, 4–5, Philipp Znidar/picture alliance, 23; Pexels/David Riaño Cortés, 9, Dayan Rodio, 16; Unsplash/Agustin Diaz Gargiulo, cover, 1, J. Balla Photography, 18, Omar Mena, 28, Raphael Nogueira, 10, Sébastien Goldberg, 12, Shot by Cerqueira, 27, 29, Thiago Sanchez, 24; Wikimedia Commons/ Arne Müseler / www.arne-mueseler.com, CC BY-SA 3.0 DE, 3, 29, Benedito Calixto, 11, Christoph, 15, Desconhecido. Colorida por Djalma Gomes Netto., 17, El Gráfico/public domain, 21, Lopo Homem, 6, Raimundo Teixeira Mendes, 8, 10, 14, 16, 20, 22, Superior Electoral Court of Brazil, 14

Library of Congress Cataloging-in-Publication Data
Names: Musolf, Nell author
Title: Brazil / Nell Musolf.
Description: Mankato, Minnesota : Creative Education and Creative Paperbacks, [2026] | Series: Spotlight on nations | Includes bibliographical references and index. | Audience: Ages 10–13 | Audience: Grades 4–6 | Summary: "Explore Brazil's history, culture, and economy, spotlighting its natural beauty, significant events, and challenges like deforestation and social inequality. Written for middle-grade readers, this book includes timelines, sidebars, glossary, resources, and index"— Provided by publisher.
Identifiers: LCCN 2025017181 (print) | LCCN 2025017182 (ebook) | ISBN 9798895810682 library binding | ISBN 9798896800217 paperback | ISBN 9798895811948 ebook
Subjects: LCSH: Brazil—History—Juvenile literature | Brazil—Politics and government—Juvenile literature
Classification: LCC F2508.5 .M87 2026 (print) | LCC F2508.5 (ebook) | DDC 981—dc23/eng/20250606
LC record available at https://lccn.loc.gov/2025017181
LC ebook record available at https://lccn.loc.gov/2025017182

Printed in the United States

CONTENTS

THE TREASURES OF
BRAZIL

Brazil is a country in South America. It is the fifth-largest country in the world. Many people live there, so many that the population of Brazil makes up one-third of the population of all Latin America! Brazil is a country rich in natural beauty and resources. It has miles of coastline along the Atlantic Ocean. It is home to the Amazon River **basin**. This basin is filled with a wide variety of plants and animals. It is also where the largest rainforest in the world exists. The Amazon rainforest plays an important role in the Earth's environment. Brazil is also filled with vibrant traditions and celebrations. It is known as a country that loves soccer, and as the home of one of the best soccer players in history. Each year, Brazil puts on the biggest carnival in the world. People come from all over to see it. The treasures of Brazil benefit the whole world.

CLOSE-UP

Borders

Brazil spans an area of about 3.3 million square miles (8.5 million square kilometers). It is so big that it borders almost all the other countries in South America. Only Chile and Ecuador don't share a border with Brazil.

CHAPTER ONE

HISTORY OF BRAZIL

People have been living in what is now known as Brazil since 9000 B.C. Back then, its name was *Pindorama*, which meant "Land of the Palms" in the **indigenous** language. The people living there were hunters, farmers, gatherers, and fishers.

Explorers from Portugal arrived in 1500 A.D. They began **colonizing** the land. They discovered a reddish wood called brazilwood. That is where Brazil gets its modern-day name. The Portuguese began cutting down brazilwood trees and sending the wood back to Europe. To continue harvesting brazilwood, the Portuguese needed workers to help. Many native workers died from diseases brought by the Europeans. Others ran away to avoid being made into slaves. The Portuguese began bringing slaves to Brazil from Africa. It wasn't until 1888 that Princess Isabel ended slavery in the country.

Toward the end of the 17th century, gold, diamonds, and emeralds were discovered in Gerais, Brazil. So much gold was found that in the late 1600s, more than 30,000 pounds (13,600 kilograms) of gold were sent to

MILESTONES IN BRAZIL'S HISTORY

1500

▸ **Portuguese arrive in Brazil and begin colonization for the Portuguese crown**

Portugal each year. A gold rush started. People from all over Europe went to Brazil to find their fortune. The gold rush lasted almost two centuries.

Brazil had other natural resources besides gold. Coffee became a big export in the 19th century. In 1820, more than 12 million pounds (5.4 million kg) of coffee were exported by Brazil. By 1850, half of the world's coffee came from Brazil. Rubber was also an important export. Selling rubber to other countries helped bring wealth to poor villages. Unfortunately, harvesting rubber plants was harmful to the Amazon jungle.

The 19th century also saw political changes in Brazil. In 1822, Brazil declared its independence from Portugal. It moved from being a colony of Portugal to its own empire. In 1889, the military took over the government

---

HISTORICAL  HIGHLIGHT

Fordlandia

In the late 1920s, Henry Ford, owner of Ford Motor Company, had an idea. He needed rubber for the tires of Ford cars. He decided to create a city called Fordlandia in Brazil, where rubber could be taken from local rubber trees at a cheaper cost to him. The city would have everything Ford's workers needed, from living quarters to schools for the employees' children. Fordlandia was completed in 1930. Problems began almost immediately. Ford had trouble finding workers and getting rubber out of the jungle. Fordlandia lasted for only a decade and was sold back to the government of Brazil after World War II.

for almost 100 years. In 1964, the country fell under a **junta**. This lasted until 1985, when the people of Brazil established a **democracy**.

Brazil in the 21st century has become a strong player in the global economy. The country continues to export goods to the rest of the world. Instead of gold and diamonds, Brazil now exports soybeans, oil, and iron ore. It is also a country with a huge amount of land. That land has many natural resources. The Amazon rainforest produces oxygen and fresh water. Brazil also has large oil and gas reserves. Despite its natural wealth, Brazil still faces problems. There is a wide gap between the wealthy and the poor. It has been a problem throughout the country's history.

1695

▸ Gold is discovered in the region now known as Minas Gerais

1776

▸ The Treaty of San Ildefonso is signed by Spain and Portugal and sets Brazil's borders

Christch the Redeemer

In Rio de Janeiro, there stands a 98-foot (30-meter) statue of Jesus Christ, savior of the Christian faith. Completed in 1931, the statue is called Christ the Redeemer and is a symbol of Christianity. The statue is considered one of the new Seven Wonders of the World.

HISTORICAL  **HIGHLIGHT**

Gold Fever

Everyone wants to find gold and become rich. When gold was discovered in the mountains of Brazil, a group of Portuguese men called "Bandeirantes" was there to lay claim to any nugget they could dig up. *Bandeirantes* means "flag carriers" in Portuguese, and these men did just that. They ventured into the mountains, claiming land for Portugal by planting the country's flag. Similar to cowboys in America, the Bandeirantes played a big part in the westward expansion of Brazil.

1807

▸ The Portuguese royal family leaves Portugal for Brazil after France invades Portugal

1822

▸ Portuguese king Peter I declares independence from Portugal and becomes emperor of Brazil

CLOSE-UP
Sugarloaf Cable Car
The Sugarloaf Cable Car in Rio de Janeiro offers stunning views of the city, beaches, and mountains. It travels in two stages, first to Morro da Urca and then to the top of Sugarloaf Mountain.

CHAPTER TWO

GOVERNMENT AND ECONOMY

When Brazil celebrated its 500th birthday in 2000, the country had gone through many changes. Brazil was ruled as a colony by the Portuguese royal family when it was first colonized in 1500. Since then, Brazil has gone from being a **monarchy** to a democracy. Brazil now has a president who is elected by the Brazilian people.

Over the years, Brazil has had several constitutions. A constitution is a set of rules for how a government is run. Brazil's current constitution is known as "the citizen constitution." It was created in 1988. The goal of the 1988 constitution was to give local governments more freedom. The local governments also gained more responsibility to make their own policies.

Brazil has a strong economy. It sells many different products to countries around the world. Brazil is one of the world's leading suppliers of food, including rice, corn, and wheat. Brazil also exports cattle and has the second-largest herd on the planet at 232 million head. Cattle in Brazil are mainly grass fed. In 2018, Brazil provided almost 20 percent of the world's beef.

1888

▸ Princess Isabel abolishes slavery in Brazil

1889

▸ Brazil becomes a republic

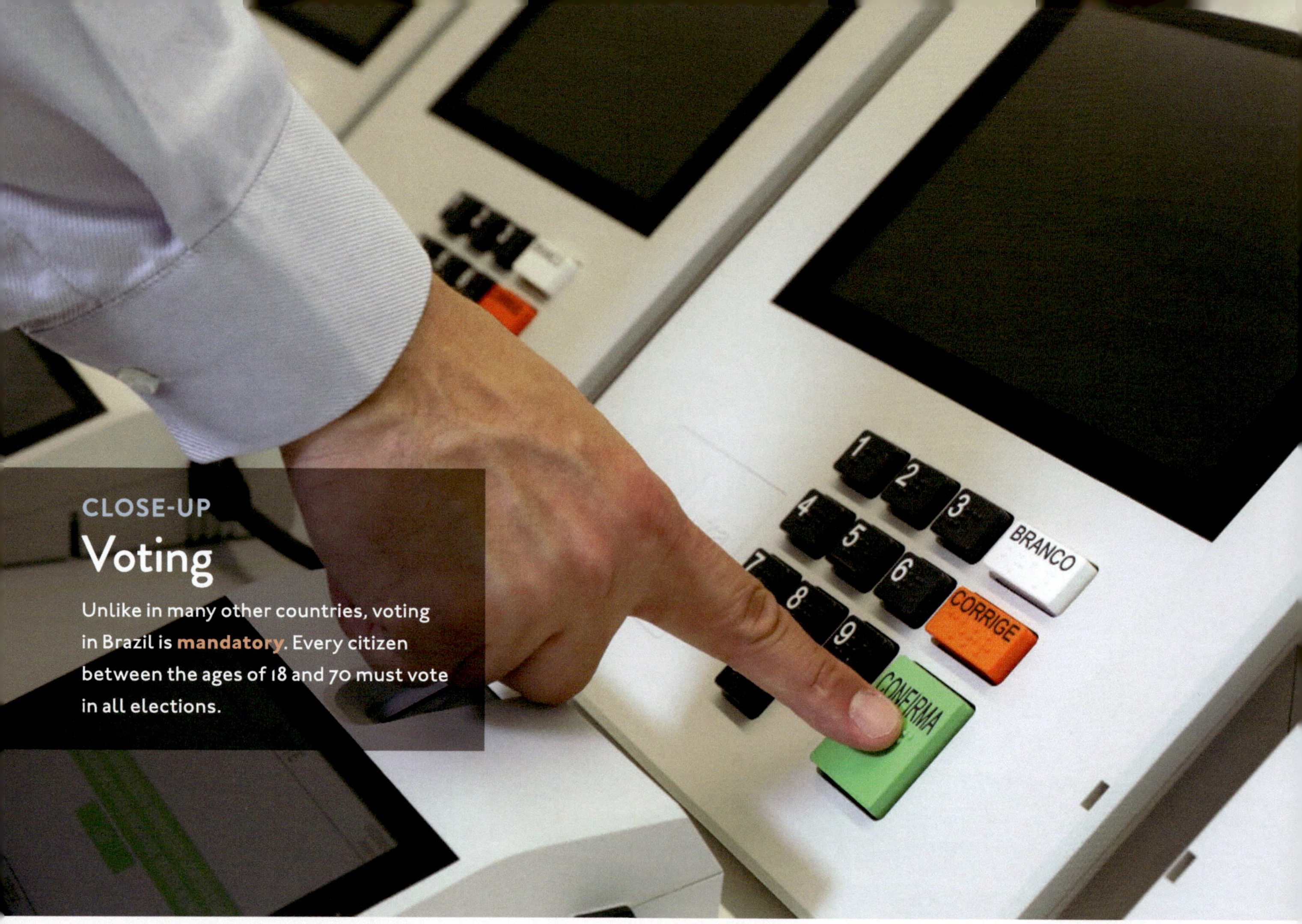

HISTORICAL HIGHLIGHT

500 Candles on the Country's Cake

The year-long celebration of Brazil's 500th birthday in 2000 got off to a bumpy start. Not everyone thought it was something to celebrate. People from Brazilian indigenous groups took part in protests and destroyed monuments. They didn't want to celebrate Portuguese colonization. They saw the anniversary as a date that began the ending of their native cultures. Historians believe there were approximately two to six million indigenous people living in Brazil when the Portuguese arrived. Now there are around 300,000.

Coffee beans continue to be one of Brazil's most popular exports. In 2023, Brazil exported 7 billion dollars worth of coffee to other countries. Brazil exports more coffee than any other country.

In 2023, Brazil took charge of The Group of 20 (G20) for one year. G20 is a group of people representing many of the world's largest economies. G20 talks about issues relating to the world's economy and other topics, including climate change.

Despite having a strong economy, the Brazilian government faces many problems and challenges. Bias against people of different races is one problem. Many people still live in poverty. Brazil also faces many environmental issues, especially the **deforestation** of the Amazon rainforest. The government has taken steps to change things. It is exploring solar and wind power as clean energy sources. New social programs have been created to help people meet basic needs.

1930

▸ Getúlio Vargas comes into power following a revolt

1943

▸ Brazil joins the Allies in World War II

Remission for Reading

Prisoners in Brazil can reduce their prison sentence by four days for every book they read. They must check out the book from the prison's library, read it within one month, and write a review.

HISTORICAL HIGHLIGHT

Coup D'etat

The government in Brazil has a long history of violence. In 1945, Brazilian president Getúlio Vargas was removed from his position by a *coup d'etat*. Coup d'etat is a French term that means the overthrowing of a government in a sudden, often violent act. A coup replaces leaders but doesn't always change a country's social or economic status. In other words, a coup d'etat changes who is working for the government, but it doesn't always change how the government works.

1945

- President Vargas is removed from office by military coup
- Brazil adopts a new constitution and returns power to the states

CLOSE-UP
Samba Style
Brazilian football is known for its flashy moves. Some people attribute those moves to samba, a popular style of music in Brazil.

CHAPTER THREE

PEOPLE, CULTURE, AND TRADITIONS

The people of Brazil come from many different cultures. They are known for their warm and friendly natures. The largest racial groups making up Brazil's population are White, Black, indigenous, and Asian. People of mixed-race, or having parents from two different races, also make up a large portion of the population. Racial discrimination is illegal in Brazil, but racism still exists.

Portuguese is the official language of Brazil. Fifty-three percent of all Brazilians are Catholic. Due to the high number of Catholics, many of the country's celebrations are religious, including the festival of São João. This festival is one of Brazil's largest annual celebrations and is held during the summer. It celebrates the end of the rainy season. Other celebrations include Réveillon, held in Rio de Janeiro to welcome the new year. The Rio Carnival, also held in Rio de Janeiro, is the most famous yearly celebration in Brazil and brings visitors in from around the world.

Brazilian families tend to be close and loving. The culture of Brazil allows more freedom for men than women. It is generally a **patriarchal** society,

1960

▸ Brasília becomes the capital of Brazil

1964

▸ A military coup overthrows the democratically elected government

although that is slowly changing. There is still a distinct line between what is considered a boy's job and what girls are expected to do. Boys and men usually take care of jobs like mowing the lawn and working on cars. Girls and women do household chores such as cleaning and cooking.

All Brazilians must attend school between the ages of 7 and 14. Public schools are often overcrowded. This is a problem especially in rural areas and poorer areas in cities. Up to three-quarters of young people do not continue school longer than they are required to by law.

After high school, students may continue their education if they want to. There are both private and public colleges. Most of the public universities are free, but students must pass challenging exams before being admitted.

For fun, Brazilians enjoy music, art, and sports—especially soccer. Soccer is the national sport of Brazil. Also known as "futebol," it is the sport that some people call the glue that holds Brazil together. The king of Brazilian

—————— HISTORICAL   HIGHLIGHT ——————

Pelé

It isn't often a person is declared a national treasure. But that is what happened to Pelé, Brazil's most famous soccer player, in 1961. Born Edson Arantes do Nascimento, the future star athlete took his nickname after mispronouncing the name of his favorite soccer player, Bilé. Pelé played for Brazil from 1956 to 1977. He was part of three Brazilian teams that won the FIFA World Cup championships in 1958, 1962, and 1970. Pelé was so beloved by his countrymen that in 2014, the Pelé Museum opened in Santos, Brazil. Pelé died in 2022, but his influence on the sport remains strong today.

1974

▸ General Ernest Geisel becomes president
▸ Reforms are introduced, reducing political activity and elections

1985

▸ Tancredo Neves is elected president but dies from medical issues before inauguration
▸ Vice president-elect José Sarney becomes president

soccer was Pelé. Pelé started playing soccer after World War II. He remains a legend and is the ideal of what a soccer player should be.

Dining in Brazil can range from steak-houses (*churrascarias*) to rice and beans (*arroz com feijoa*). People like to use native fruits such as guava and coconut in drinks. Coffee is a popular beverage for adults. The national dish of Brazil is feijoada, a thick stew made with black beans and pork. The dish's history goes back to the days of slavery when slaves made meals out of leftovers and beans. Feijoada is still an economic dish for many people and has become part of Brazil's culture.

Sweet Tooth

Brazil has many sugar cane plantations. With so much sweetness on hand, many local recipes use a lot of sugar along with other natural resources, including coconut milk and palm oil.

HISTORICAL  **HIGHLIGHT**

Rio Carnival

The history of the famous Rio Carnival stretches back to 1723. Back then, Portuguese immigrants wandered the streets throwing buckets of water along with mud and food at each other. The carnival has come a long way since then with parades, street parties, and fancy balls. Now, it has become possibly the best-known carnival in the world. Millions flock to Rio de Janeiro to join in on the events. The carnival traditionally takes place in February before Ash Wednesday. Ash Wednesday marks the beginning of **Lent** for many Christian faiths. Called by some "The Greatest Show on Earth," the Rio Carnival is filled with music, food, fireworks, and people.

1988

▸ Brazil adopts a new constitution that reduces presidential powers

1997

▸ Brazil's constitution is changed to allow presidents to run for reelection

BRAZIL TODAY

As the largest country in South America, and the fifth largest country in the world, Brazil is a nation of global importance. Brazil supplies the rest of the world with many products. It is the world's biggest exporter of soybeans, raw sugar, frozen beef, poultry meat, and coffee.

Brazil is also home to the largest portion of the Amazon rainforest. The Amazon covers about one percent of the planet's surface. It contains ten percent of all known wildlife species. Hundreds of different kinds of birds, alligators, snakes, and mammals live along the banks of the Amazon River. In the water are manatees, freshwater dolphins, and 450 kinds of catfish. Scientists believe there are possibly hundreds or even thousands of unknown plant and animal species in the Amazon basin. They believe more species will be discovered in time.

Unfortunately, the Amazon rainforest is under constant threat from both humans and nature. Deforestation, climate change, and fires are destroying huge areas of the rainforest. Once a section of the rainforest is

2004

▸ Brazil launches its first space rocket

2010

▸ Dilma Rousseff becomes Brazil's first woman president

Deforestation

gone, it can't be brought back. Ranching and farming are also using up acres of land. Discovering ways to save the rainforest from further destruction is a problem for not only Brazil, but also for the entire planet.

In addition to environmental issues, Brazil has many economic challenges. There has always been a wide difference between the wealthy and the poor in Brazil. As of 2024, this difference reached new extreme levels. Most of the wealth remains in the top one percent of Brazilian citizens. Many of the poor continue to live in poverty. Although Brazil has one of the largest economies in the world, trying to make the economy more equitable is a challenge the country may face for years to come.

Brazil is a nation that has withstood centuries of change. But one thing that remains the same is the pride its people have for their country. Despite facing many difficulties, Brazil's people continue to work toward a better future for their beloved nation.

2016

▸ Senate approves 20-year spending freeze aimed at restoring economic health to Brazil

2023

▸ Luiz Inácio Lula da Silva becomes president for the third time, 12 years after his first two terms as president

BRAZIL

Continent: South America

Capital city: Brasília

Population: 212.5 million

Official language: Portuguese

Type of government: Democracy

Currency: Brazilian real

Main religion practiced: Roman Catholicism

Colors on flag: Green, yellow, blue

National animal: Jaguar

WORDS to Know

basin — an area of land around a river from which water drains into the river

colonize — to establish political control over another place

deforestation — the clearing or cutting down of forests

democracy — a system of government in which people choose their leaders in elections

ecosystem — a community of animals and plants interacting with their environment

indigenous — the first people to live in a place

junta — a group of people controlling a government after a revolution

Lent — a period of 40 days in which Christians prepare for Easter, usually by fasting

mandatory — required by law

monarchy — a system of government in which one person has complete control

patriarchal — relating to a system of society controlled by men

LEARN MORE

Books

Abramson, Marcia. *South America*. Minneapolis: Bearport Publishing, 2024.

Barry, James. *Brazil*. Mankato, Minn.: Creative Education and Creative Paperbacks, 2026.

Dickmann, Nancy. *Your Passport to Brazil*. North Mankato, Minn.: Capstone Press, 2023.

Websites

"Brazil Facts for Kids." Science Kids.

https://www.sciencekids.co.nz/sciencefacts/countries/brazil.html

"Brazil Facts: Learn about this Cool Country!" National Geographic Kids.

https://www.natgeokids.com/uk/discover/geography/countries/country-fact-file-brazil/

"Virtual Travel: Brazil." Global Citizens Club for Kids.

https://www.packmoreintolife.com/global-citizens-club-for-kids-virtual-trip-to-brazil-brazilian-arts-and-crafts-for-kids/

Documentaries

Czajka, Chris, dir. *Time for School: Brazil*. New York: Thirteen/WNET, 2016.

Pritz, Alex, dir. *The Territory*. New York: Documist, 2022.

Wynn, Steve, dir. *Passport to Brazil*. Springfield, Mo.: Ozarks Public Television, 2017.

Note: Every effort has been made to ensure that any websites listed above were active at the time of publication. However, because of the nature of the Internet, it is impossible to guarantee that these sites will remain active indefinitely or that their contents will not be altered.

Visit

BETO CARRERO WORLD

Latin America's largest amusement park has rides, a zoo, and entertainment for the whole family.
Armaçáo, Penha
Santa Catarina, Brazil

CHRIST THE REDEEMER

Visit one of Brazil's most famous landmarks by foot, van, or train and take in the spectacular view from the top of Corcovado Mountain.
Paruqe Nacional da Tijuca
Rio de Janeiro, Brazil

MUSEU DO AMANHÁ (MUSEUM OF TOMORROW)

This experimental museum combines science with art and technology to explore the future of the planet and society.
Praça Mauá, 1 – Centro
Rio de Janeiro, Brazil

ZOO SÃO PAULO

The largest zoo in Latin America, Zoo São Paulo features animals native to Brazil such as jaguars and Guianan cocks-of-the-rock.
Avenida Miguel Estefno, 4241 – Água Funda
São Paulo, Brazil

INDEX